EVERYONE IS WELCOME

RECORD BOOK

NAME ______________________________

SCHOOL ______________________________

GRADE/SUBJECT ______________________________

ROOM ______________________________

SCHOOL YEAR ______________________________

SCHOOL ADDRESS ______________________________

SCHOOL PHONE ______________________________

CONTENTS

Teacher Created Resources
12621 Western Avenue
Garden Grove, CA 92841
www.teachercreated.com
ISBN: 978-1-4206-0687-4

Reprinted, 2023
Made in U.S.A.

Teacher Created Resources

Editor in Chief: Brent L. Fox, M. Ed.
Creative Director: Sarah M. Fournier
Cover Design: Denise Bauer
Imaging: Diem Pascarella
Publisher: Mary D. Smith, M.S. Ed.

HOW TO USE THE RECORD BOOK

MONTHLY REMINDERS (page 3)

Use this chart as a quick reference. Record significant events, meetings, appointments, conferences, seminars, etc.

STUDENT ROSTER (pages 4–5)

Record both student and parent or guardian names and addresses. Where applicable, make a special note of differences in last names. You may wish to list siblings and their grades if they attend the same school. Notes may include information regarding special needs and any necessary medications.

WEEKLY RECORDS (pages 6–63)

The weekly record section is designed to provide organized space for recording daily notations or grades for assignments, tests, attendance, tardies, participation, etc. Each page contains a five-week block of spaces so that a student's record for an entire quarter of ten weeks can be read on facing pages. Summary columns for recording total attendance, tardies, and other information appear on the right-hand facing page for each ten-week period.

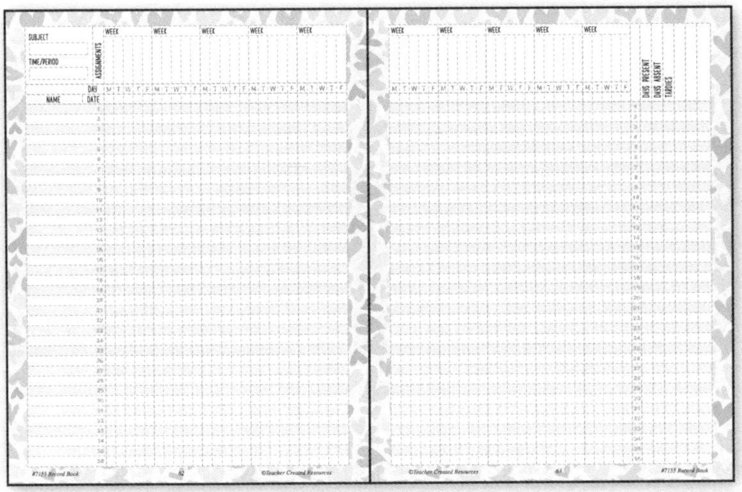

GRADING CHART (page 64)

A convenient chart for scoring students' work is provided at the back of this book. Use the chart as a quick reference when scoring 3 to 50 items of equal value. To use the chart, simply "connect" the row that matches the total number of items to be scored with the column indicating the number of incorrect items.

By following across the row and up the column to the intersection point (number), you can determine the raw score. For example, if the total number of items on a given test is 35, and a student marked 5 incorrectly, his or her score would be 86%. The score is obtained by moving across row 35 and up column 5 to the point where they meet (86%).

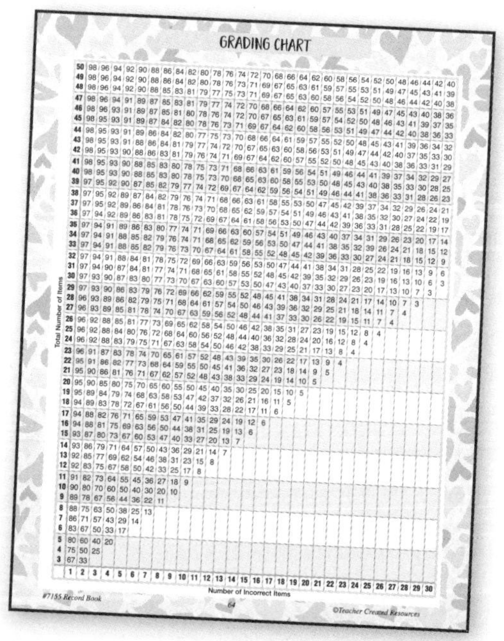

MONTHLY REMINDERS

DATE	JULY	DATE	AUGUST
DATE	SEPTEMBER	DATE	OCTOBER
DATE	NOVEMBER	DATE	DECEMBER
DATE	JANUARY	DATE	FEBRUARY
DATE	MARCH	DATE	APRIL
DATE	MAY	DATE	JUNE

STUDENT ROSTER

STUDENT	PARENT/GUARDIAN	ADDRESS
1.		
2.		
3.		
4.		
5.		
6.		
7.		
8.		
9.		
10.		
11.		
12.		
13.		
14.		
15.		
16.		
17.		
18.		
19.		
20.		
21.		
22.		
23.		
24.		
25.		
26.		
27.		
28.		
29.		
30.		
31.		
32.		
33.		
34.		
35.		
36.		

STUDENT ROSTER

WORK/HOME PHONE	SIBLINGS	NOTES

SUBJECT

TIME/PERIOD

ASSIGNMENTS		WEEK					WEEK					WEEK					WEEK					WEEK				
	DAY	M	T	W	T	F	M	T	W	T	F	M	T	W	T	F	M	T	W	T	F	M	T	W	T	F
NAME	DATE																									
	1																									
	2																									
	3																									
	4																									
	5																									
	6																									
	7																									
	8																									
	9																									
	10																									
	11																									
	12																									
	13																									
	14																									
	15																									
	16																									
	17																									
	18																									
	19																									
	20																									
	21																									
	22																									
	23																									
	24																									
	25																									
	26																									
	27																									
	28																									
	29																									
	30																									
	31																									
	32																									
	33																									
	34																									
	35																									
	36																									

WEEK					WEEK					WEEK					WEEK					WEEK						DAYS PRESENT	DAYS ABSENT	TARDIES			
M	T	W	T	F	M	T	W	T	F	M	T	W	T	F	M	T	W	T	F	M	T	W	T	F							
																									1						
																									2						
																									3						
																									4						
																									5						
																									6						
																									7						
																									8						
																									9						
																									10						
																									11						
																									12						
																									13						
																									14						
																									15						
																									16						
																									17						
																									18						
																									19						
																									20						
																									21						
																									22						
																									23						
																									24						
																									25						
																									26						
																									27						
																									28						
																									29						
																									30						
																									31						
																									32						
																									33						
																									34						
																									35						
																									36						

SUBJECT

TIME/PERIOD

	ASSIGNMENTS	WEEK					WEEK					WEEK					WEEK					WEEK				
	DAY	M	T	W	T	F	M	T	W	T	F	M	T	W	T	F	M	T	W	T	F	M	T	W	T	F
NAME	DATE																									
	1																									
	2																									
	3																									
	4																									
	5																									
	6																									
	7																									
	8																									
	9																									
	10																									
	11																									
	12																									
	13																									
	14																									
	15																									
	16																									
	17																									
	18																									
	19																									
	20																									
	21																									
	22																									
	23																									
	24																									
	25																									
	26																									
	27																									
	28																									
	29																									
	30																									
	31																									
	32																									
	33																									
	34																									
	35																									
	36																									

WEEK					WEEK					WEEK					WEEK					WEEK						DAYS PRESENT	DAYS ABSENT	TARDIES			
M	T	W	T	F	M	T	W	T	F	M	T	W	T	F	M	T	W	T	F	M	T	W	T	F							
																									1						
																									2						
																									3						
																									4						
																									5						
																									6						
																									7						
																									8						
																									9						
																									10						
																									11						
																									12						
																									13						
																									14						
																									15						
																									16						
																									17						
																									18						
																									19						
																									20						
																									21						
																									22						
																									23						
																									24						
																									25						
																									26						
																									27						
																									28						
																									29						
																									30						
																									31						
																									32						
																									33						
																									34						
																									35						
																									36						

SUBJECT TIME/PERIOD	ASSIGNMENTS	WEEK					WEEK					WEEK					WEEK					WEEK				
	DAY	M	T	W	T	F	M	T	W	T	F	M	T	W	T	F	M	T	W	T	F	M	T	W	T	F
NAME	DATE																									
	1																									
	2																									
	3																									
	4																									
	5																									
	6																									
	7																									
	8																									
	9																									
	10																									
	11																									
	12																									
	13																									
	14																									
	15																									
	16																									
	17																									
	18																									
	19																									
	20																									
	21																									
	22																									
	23																									
	24																									
	25																									
	26																									
	27																									
	28																									
	29																									
	30																									
	31																									
	32																									
	33																									
	34																									
	35																									
	36																									

WEEK					WEEK					WEEK					WEEK					WEEK						DAYS PRESENT	DAYS ABSENT	TARDIES			
M	T	W	T	F	M	T	W	T	F	M	T	W	T	F	M	T	W	T	F	M	T	W	T	F							
																									1						
																									2						
																									3						
																									4						
																									5						
																									6						
																									7						
																									8						
																									9						
																									10						
																									11						
																									12						
																									13						
																									14						
																									15						
																									16						
																									17						
																									18						
																									19						
																									20						
																									21						
																									22						
																									23						
																									24						
																									25						
																									26						
																									27						
																									28						
																									29						
																									30						
																									31						
																									32						
																									33						
																									34						
																									35						
																									36						

SUBJECT TIME/PERIOD	ASSIGNMENTS	WEEK					WEEK					WEEK					WEEK					WEEK				
	DAY	M	T	W	T	F	M	T	W	T	F	M	T	W	T	F	M	T	W	T	F	M	T	W	T	F
NAME	DATE																									
	1																									
	2																									
	3																									
	4																									
	5																									
	6																									
	7																									
	8																									
	9																									
	10																									
	11																									
	12																									
	13																									
	14																									
	15																									
	16																									
	17																									
	18																									
	19																									
	20																									
	21																									
	22																									
	23																									
	24																									
	25																									
	26																									
	27																									
	28																									
	29																									
	30																									
	31																									
	32																									
	33																									
	34																									
	35																									
	36																									

WEEK					WEEK					WEEK					WEEK					WEEK						DAYS PRESENT	DAYS ABSENT	TARDIES			
M	T	W	T	F	M	T	W	T	F	M	T	W	T	F	M	T	W	T	F	M	T	W	T	F							
																									1						
																									2						
																									3						
																									4						
																									5						
																									6						
																									7						
																									8						
																									9						
																									10						
																									11						
																									12						
																									13						
																									14						
																									15						
																									16						
																									17						
																									18						
																									19						
																									20						
																									21						
																									22						
																									23						
																									24						
																									25						
																									26						
																									27						
																									28						
																									29						
																									30						
																									31						
																									32						
																									33						
																									34						
																									35						
																									36						

SUBJECT TIME/PERIOD	ASSIGNMENTS	WEEK					WEEK					WEEK					WEEK					WEEK				
	DAY	M	T	W	T	F	M	T	W	T	F	M	T	W	T	F	M	T	W	T	F	M	T	W	T	F
NAME	DATE																									
	1																									
	2																									
	3																									
	4																									
	5																									
	6																									
	7																									
	8																									
	9																									
	10																									
	11																									
	12																									
	13																									
	14																									
	15																									
	16																									
	17																									
	18																									
	19																									
	20																									
	21																									
	22																									
	23																									
	24																									
	25																									
	26																									
	27																									
	28																									
	29																									
	30																									
	31																									
	32																									
	33																									
	34																									
	35																									
	36																									

| WEEK | | | | | WEEK | | | | | WEEK | | | | | WEEK | | | | | WEEK | | | | | | | | | | | |
M	T	W	T	F	M	T	W	T	F	M	T	W	T	F	M	T	W	T	F	M	T	W	T	F		DAYS PRESENT	DAYS ABSENT	TARDIES			
																									1						
																									2						
																									3						
																									4						
																									5						
																									6						
																									7						
																									8						
																									9						
																									10						
																									11						
																									12						
																									13						
																									14						
																									15						
																									16						
																									17						
																									18						
																									19						
																									20						
																									21						
																									22						
																									23						
																									24						
																									25						
																									26						
																									27						
																									28						
																									29						
																									30						
																									31						
																									32						
																									33						
																									34						
																									35						
																									36						

SUBJECT

TIME/PERIOD

	ASSIGNMENTS	WEEK					WEEK					WEEK					WEEK					WEEK				
	DAY	M	T	W	T	F	M	T	W	T	F	M	T	W	T	F	M	T	W	T	F	M	T	W	T	F
NAME	DATE																									
	1																									
	2																									
	3																									
	4																									
	5																									
	6																									
	7																									
	8																									
	9																									
	10																									
	11																									
	12																									
	13																									
	14																									
	15																									
	16																									
	17																									
	18																									
	19																									
	20																									
	21																									
	22																									
	23																									
	24																									
	25																									
	26																									
	27																									
	28																									
	29																									
	30																									
	31																									
	32																									
	33																									
	34																									
	35																									
	36																									

WEEK					WEEK					WEEK					WEEK					WEEK						DAYS PRESENT	DAYS ABSENT	TARDIES			
M	T	W	T	F	M	T	W	T	F	M	T	W	T	F	M	T	W	T	F	M	T	W	T	F							
																									1						
																									2						
																									3						
																									4						
																									5						
																									6						
																									7						
																									8						
																									9						
																									10						
																									11						
																									12						
																									13						
																									14						
																									15						
																									16						
																									17						
																									18						
																									19						
																									20						
																									21						
																									22						
																									23						
																									24						
																									25						
																									26						
																									27						
																									28						
																									29						
																									30						
																									31						
																									32						
																									33						
																									34						
																									35						
																									36						

SUBJECT

TIME/PERIOD

ASSIGNMENTS		WEEK					WEEK					WEEK					WEEK					WEEK				
	DAY	M	T	W	T	F	M	T	W	T	F	M	T	W	T	F	M	T	W	T	F	M	T	W	T	F
NAME	DATE																									
	1																									
	2																									
	3																									
	4																									
	5																									
	6																									
	7																									
	8																									
	9																									
	10																									
	11																									
	12																									
	13																									
	14																									
	15																									
	16																									
	17																									
	18																									
	19																									
	20																									
	21																									
	22																									
	23																									
	24																									
	25																									
	26																									
	27																									
	28																									
	29																									
	30																									
	31																									
	32																									
	33																									
	34																									
	35																									
	36																									

WEEK					WEEK					WEEK					WEEK					WEEK						DAYS PRESENT	DAYS ABSENT	TARDIES			
M	T	W	T	F	M	T	W	T	F	M	T	W	T	F	M	T	W	T	F	M	T	W	T	F							
																									1						
																									2						
																									3						
																									4						
																									5						
																									6						
																									7						
																									8						
																									9						
																									10						
																									11						
																									12						
																									13						
																									14						
																									15						
																									16						
																									17						
																									18						
																									19						
																									20						
																									21						
																									22						
																									23						
																									24						
																									25						
																									26						
																									27						
																									28						
																									29						
																									30						
																									31						
																									32						
																									33						
																									34						
																									35						
																									36						

SUBJECT

TIME/PERIOD

	ASSIGNMENTS	WEEK					WEEK					WEEK					WEEK					WEEK				
	DAY	M	T	W	T	F	M	T	W	T	F	M	T	W	T	F	M	T	W	T	F	M	T	W	T	F
NAME	DATE																									
	1																									
	2																									
	3																									
	4																									
	5																									
	6																									
	7																									
	8																									
	9																									
	10																									
	11																									
	12																									
	13																									
	14																									
	15																									
	16																									
	17																									
	18																									
	19																									
	20																									
	21																									
	22																									
	23																									
	24																									
	25																									
	26																									
	27																									
	28																									
	29																									
	30																									
	31																									
	32																									
	33																									
	34																									
	35																									
	36																									

WEEK					WEEK					WEEK					WEEK					WEEK						DAYS PRESENT	DAYS ABSENT	TARDIES			
M	T	W	T	F	M	T	W	T	F	M	T	W	T	F	M	T	W	T	F	M	T	W	T	F							
																									1						
																									2						
																									3						
																									4						
																									5						
																									6						
																									7						
																									8						
																									9						
																									10						
																									11						
																									12						
																									13						
																									14						
																									15						
																									16						
																									17						
																									18						
																									19						
																									20						
																									21						
																									22						
																									23						
																									24						
																									25						
																									26						
																									27						
																									28						
																									29						
																									30						
																									31						
																									32						
																									33						
																									34						
																									35						
																									36						

SUBJECT / TIME/PERIOD	ASSIGNMENTS	WEEK					WEEK					WEEK					WEEK					WEEK				
	DAY	M	T	W	T	F	M	T	W	T	F	M	T	W	T	F	M	T	W	T	F	M	T	W	T	F
NAME	DATE																									
	1																									
	2																									
	3																									
	4																									
	5																									
	6																									
	7																									
	8																									
	9																									
	10																									
	11																									
	12																									
	13																									
	14																									
	15																									
	16																									
	17																									
	18																									
	19																									
	20																									
	21																									
	22																									
	23																									
	24																									
	25																									
	26																									
	27																									
	28																									
	29																									
	30																									
	31																									
	32																									
	33																									
	34																									
	35																									
	36																									

WEEK					WEEK					WEEK					WEEK					WEEK						DAYS PRESENT	DAYS ABSENT	TARDIES			
M	T	W	T	F	M	T	W	T	F	M	T	W	T	F	M	T	W	T	F	M	T	W	T	F							
																									1						
																									2						
																									3						
																									4						
																									5						
																									6						
																									7						
																									8						
																									9						
																									10						
																									11						
																									12						
																									13						
																									14						
																									15						
																									16						
																									17						
																									18						
																									19						
																									20						
																									21						
																									22						
																									23						
																									24						
																									25						
																									26						
																									27						
																									28						
																									29						
																									30						
																									31						
																									32						
																									33						
																									34						
																									35						
																									36						

SUBJECT

TIME/PERIOD

	ASSIGNMENTS	WEEK					WEEK					WEEK					WEEK					WEEK				
	DAY	M	T	W	T	F	M	T	W	T	F	M	T	W	T	F	M	T	W	T	F	M	T	W	T	F
NAME	DATE																									
	1																									
	2																									
	3																									
	4																									
	5																									
	6																									
	7																									
	8																									
	9																									
	10																									
	11																									
	12																									
	13																									
	14																									
	15																									
	16																									
	17																									
	18																									
	19																									
	20																									
	21																									
	22																									
	23																									
	24																									
	25																									
	26																									
	27																									
	28																									
	29																									
	30																									
	31																									
	32																									
	33																									
	34																									
	35																									
	36																									

WEEK					WEEK					WEEK					WEEK					WEEK						DAYS PRESENT	DAYS ABSENT	TARDIES			
M	T	W	T	F	M	T	W	T	F	M	T	W	T	F	M	T	W	T	F	M	T	W	T	F							
																									1						
																									2						
																									3						
																									4						
																									5						
																									6						
																									7						
																									8						
																									9						
																									10						
																									11						
																									12						
																									13						
																									14						
																									15						
																									16						
																									17						
																									18						
																									19						
																									20						
																									21						
																									22						
																									23						
																									24						
																									25						
																									26						
																									27						
																									28						
																									29						
																									30						
																									31						
																									32						
																									33						
																									34						
																									35						
																									36						

SUBJECT TIME/PERIOD	ASSIGNMENTS	WEEK					WEEK					WEEK					WEEK					WEEK				
	DAY	M	T	W	T	F	M	T	W	T	F	M	T	W	T	F	M	T	W	T	F	M	T	W	T	F
NAME	DATE																									
	1																									
	2																									
	3																									
	4																									
	5																									
	6																									
	7																									
	8																									
	9																									
	10																									
	11																									
	12																									
	13																									
	14																									
	15																									
	16																									
	17																									
	18																									
	19																									
	20																									
	21																									
	22																									
	23																									
	24																									
	25																									
	26																									
	27																									
	28																									
	29																									
	30																									
	31																									
	32																									
	33																									
	34																									
	35																									
	36																									

WEEK					WEEK					WEEK					WEEK					WEEK						DAYS PRESENT	DAYS ABSENT	TARDIES			
M	T	W	T	F	M	T	W	T	F	M	T	W	T	F	M	T	W	T	F	M	T	W	T	F							
																									1						
																									2						
																									3						
																									4						
																									5						
																									6						
																									7						
																									8						
																									9						
																									10						
																									11						
																									12						
																									13						
																									14						
																									15						
																									16						
																									17						
																									18						
																									19						
																									20						
																									21						
																									22						
																									23						
																									24						
																									25						
																									26						
																									27						
																									28						
																									29						
																									30						
																									31						
																									32						
																									33						
																									34						
																									35						
																									36						

SUBJECT

TIME/PERIOD

	ASSIGNMENTS	WEEK					WEEK					WEEK					WEEK					WEEK				
	DAY	M	T	W	T	F	M	T	W	T	F	M	T	W	T	F	M	T	W	T	F	M	T	W	T	F
NAME	DATE																									
	1																									
	2																									
	3																									
	4																									
	5																									
	6																									
	7																									
	8																									
	9																									
	10																									
	11																									
	12																									
	13																									
	14																									
	15																									
	16																									
	17																									
	18																									
	19																									
	20																									
	21																									
	22																									
	23																									
	24																									
	25																									
	26																									
	27																									
	28																									
	29																									
	30																									
	31																									
	32																									
	33																									
	34																									
	35																									
	36																									

WEEK					WEEK					WEEK					WEEK					WEEK						DAYS PRESENT	DAYS ABSENT	TARDIES			
M	T	W	T	F	M	T	W	T	F	M	T	W	T	F	M	T	W	T	F	M	T	W	T	F							
																									1						
																									2						
																									3						
																									4						
																									5						
																									6						
																									7						
																									8						
																									9						
																									10						
																									11						
																									12						
																									13						
																									14						
																									15						
																									16						
																									17						
																									18						
																									19						
																									20						
																									21						
																									22						
																									23						
																									24						
																									25						
																									26						
																									27						
																									28						
																									29						
																									30						
																									31						
																									32						
																									33						
																									34						
																									35						
																									36						

SUBJECT TIME/PERIOD	ASSIGNMENTS	WEEK					WEEK					WEEK					WEEK					WEEK				
	DAY	M	T	W	T	F	M	T	W	T	F	M	T	W	T	F	M	T	W	T	F	M	T	W	T	F
NAME	DATE																									
	1																									
	2																									
	3																									
	4																									
	5																									
	6																									
	7																									
	8																									
	9																									
	10																									
	11																									
	12																									
	13																									
	14																									
	15																									
	16																									
	17																									
	18																									
	19																									
	20																									
	21																									
	22																									
	23																									
	24																									
	25																									
	26																									
	27																									
	28																									
	29																									
	30																									
	31																									
	32																									
	33																									
	34																									
	35																									
	36																									

WEEK					WEEK					WEEK					WEEK					WEEK						DAYS PRESENT	DAYS ABSENT	TARDIES			
M	T	W	T	F	M	T	W	T	F	M	T	W	T	F	M	T	W	T	F	M	T	W	T	F							
																									1						
																									2						
																									3						
																									4						
																									5						
																									6						
																									7						
																									8						
																									9						
																									10						
																									11						
																									12						
																									13						
																									14						
																									15						
																									16						
																									17						
																									18						
																									19						
																									20						
																									21						
																									22						
																									23						
																									24						
																									25						
																									26						
																									27						
																									28						
																									29						
																									30						
																									31						
																									32						
																									33						
																									34						
																									35						
																									36						

SUBJECT

TIME/PERIOD

	ASSIGNMENTS	WEEK					WEEK					WEEK					WEEK					WEEK				
	DAY	M	T	W	T	F	M	T	W	T	F	M	T	W	T	F	M	T	W	T	F	M	T	W	T	F
NAME	DATE																									
	1																									
	2																									
	3																									
	4																									
	5																									
	6																									
	7																									
	8																									
	9																									
	10																									
	11																									
	12																									
	13																									
	14																									
	15																									
	16																									
	17																									
	18																									
	19																									
	20																									
	21																									
	22																									
	23																									
	24																									
	25																									
	26																									
	27																									
	28																									
	29																									
	30																									
	31																									
	32																									
	33																									
	34																									
	35																									
	36																									

WEEK					WEEK					WEEK					WEEK					WEEK						DAYS PRESENT	DAYS ABSENT	TARDIES			
M	T	W	T	F	M	T	W	T	F	M	T	W	T	F	M	T	W	T	F	M	T	W	T	F							
																									1						
																									2						
																									3						
																									4						
																									5						
																									6						
																									7						
																									8						
																									9						
																									10						
																									11						
																									12						
																									13						
																									14						
																									15						
																									16						
																									17						
																									18						
																									19						
																									20						
																									21						
																									22						
																									23						
																									24						
																									25						
																									26						
																									27						
																									28						
																									29						
																									30						
																									31						
																									32						
																									33						
																									34						
																									35						
																									36						

SUBJECT

TIME/PERIOD

	ASSIGNMENTS	WEEK					WEEK					WEEK					WEEK					WEEK				
	DAY	M	T	W	T	F	M	T	W	T	F	M	T	W	T	F	M	T	W	T	F	M	T	W	T	F
NAME	DATE																									
	1																									
	2																									
	3																									
	4																									
	5																									
	6																									
	7																									
	8																									
	9																									
	10																									
	11																									
	12																									
	13																									
	14																									
	15																									
	16																									
	17																									
	18																									
	19																									
	20																									
	21																									
	22																									
	23																									
	24																									
	25																									
	26																									
	27																									
	28																									
	29																									
	30																									
	31																									
	32																									
	33																									
	34																									
	35																									
	36																									

WEEK					WEEK					WEEK					WEEK					WEEK											
M	T	W	T	F	M	T	W	T	F	M	T	W	T	F	M	T	W	T	F	M	T	W	T	F		DAYS PRESENT	DAYS ABSENT	TARDIES			
																									1						
																									2						
																									3						
																									4						
																									5						
																									6						
																									7						
																									8						
																									9						
																									10						
																									11						
																									12						
																									13						
																									14						
																									15						
																									16						
																									17						
																									18						
																									19						
																									20						
																									21						
																									22						
																									23						
																									24						
																									25						
																									26						
																									27						
																									28						
																									29						
																									30						
																									31						
																									32						
																									33						
																									34						
																									35						
																									36						

SUBJECT

TIME/PERIOD

ASSIGNMENTS

		WEEK					WEEK					WEEK					WEEK					WEEK				
	DAY	M	T	W	T	F	M	T	W	T	F	M	T	W	T	F	M	T	W	T	F	M	T	W	T	F
NAME	DATE																									
	1																									
	2																									
	3																									
	4																									
	5																									
	6																									
	7																									
	8																									
	9																									
	10																									
	11																									
	12																									
	13																									
	14																									
	15																									
	16																									
	17																									
	18																									
	19																									
	20																									
	21																									
	22																									
	23																									
	24																									
	25																									
	26																									
	27																									
	28																									
	29																									
	30																									
	31																									
	32																									
	33																									
	34																									
	35																									
	36																									

WEEK					WEEK					WEEK					WEEK					WEEK						DAYS PRESENT	DAYS ABSENT	TARDIES				
M	T	W	T	F	M	T	W	T	F	M	T	W	T	F	M	T	W	T	F	M	T	W	T	F								
																									1							
																									2							
																									3							
																									4							
																									5							
																									6							
																									7							
																									8							
																									9							
																									10							
																									11							
																									12							
																									13							
																									14							
																									15							
																									16							
																									17							
																									18							
																									19							
																									20							
																									21							
																									22							
																									23							
																									24							
																									25							
																									26							
																									27							
																									28							
																									29							
																									30							
																									31							
																									32							
																									33							
																									34							
																									35							
																									36							

SUBJECT

TIME/PERIOD

ASSIGNMENTS		WEEK					WEEK					WEEK					WEEK					WEEK				
	DAY	M	T	W	T	F	M	T	W	T	F	M	T	W	T	F	M	T	W	T	F	M	T	W	T	F
NAME	DATE																									
	1																									
	2																									
	3																									
	4																									
	5																									
	6																									
	7																									
	8																									
	9																									
	10																									
	11																									
	12																									
	13																									
	14																									
	15																									
	16																									
	17																									
	18																									
	19																									
	20																									
	21																									
	22																									
	23																									
	24																									
	25																									
	26																									
	27																									
	28																									
	29																									
	30																									
	31																									
	32																									
	33																									
	34																									
	35																									
	36																									

WEEK					WEEK					WEEK					WEEK					WEEK						DAYS PRESENT	DAYS ABSENT	TARDIES			
M	T	W	T	F	M	T	W	T	F	M	T	W	T	F	M	T	W	T	F	M	T	W	T	F							
																									1						
																									2						
																									3						
																									4						
																									5						
																									6						
																									7						
																									8						
																									9						
																									10						
																									11						
																									12						
																									13						
																									14						
																									15						
																									16						
																									17						
																									18						
																									19						
																									20						
																									21						
																									22						
																									23						
																									24						
																									25						
																									26						
																									27						
																									28						
																									29						
																									30						
																									31						
																									32						
																									33						
																									34						
																									35						
																									36						

SUBJECT

TIME/PERIOD

	ASSIGNMENTS	WEEK					WEEK					WEEK					WEEK					WEEK				
	DAY	M	T	W	T	F	M	T	W	T	F	M	T	W	T	F	M	T	W	T	F	M	T	W	T	F
NAME	DATE																									
	1																									
	2																									
	3																									
	4																									
	5																									
	6																									
	7																									
	8																									
	9																									
	10																									
	11																									
	12																									
	13																									
	14																									
	15																									
	16																									
	17																									
	18																									
	19																									
	20																									
	21																									
	22																									
	23																									
	24																									
	25																									
	26																									
	27																									
	28																									
	29																									
	30																									
	31																									
	32																									
	33																									
	34																									
	35																									
	36																									

WEEK					WEEK					WEEK					WEEK					WEEK						DAYS PRESENT	DAYS ABSENT	TARDIES			
M	T	W	T	F	M	T	W	T	F	M	T	W	T	F	M	T	W	T	F	M	T	W	T	F							
																									1						
																									2						
																									3						
																									4						
																									5						
																									6						
																									7						
																									8						
																									9						
																									10						
																									11						
																									12						
																									13						
																									14						
																									15						
																									16						
																									17						
																									18						
																									19						
																									20						
																									21						
																									22						
																									23						
																									24						
																									25						
																									26						
																									27						
																									28						
																									29						
																									30						
																									31						
																									32						
																									33						
																									34						
																									35						
																									36						

SUBJECT

TIME/PERIOD

	ASSIGNMENTS	WEEK					WEEK					WEEK					WEEK					WEEK				
	DAY	M	T	W	T	F	M	T	W	T	F	M	T	W	T	F	M	T	W	T	F	M	T	W	T	F
NAME	DATE																									
	1																									
	2																									
	3																									
	4																									
	5																									
	6																									
	7																									
	8																									
	9																									
	10																									
	11																									
	12																									
	13																									
	14																									
	15																									
	16																									
	17																									
	18																									
	19																									
	20																									
	21																									
	22																									
	23																									
	24																									
	25																									
	26																									
	27																									
	28																									
	29																									
	30																									
	31																									
	32																									
	33																									
	34																									
	35																									
	36																									

WEEK					WEEK					WEEK					WEEK					WEEK						DAYS PRESENT	DAYS ABSENT	TARDIES			
M	T	W	T	F	M	T	W	T	F	M	T	W	T	F	M	T	W	T	F	M	T	W	T	F							
																									1						
																									2						
																									3						
																									4						
																									5						
																									6						
																									7						
																									8						
																									9						
																									10						
																									11						
																									12						
																									13						
																									14						
																									15						
																									16						
																									17						
																									18						
																									19						
																									20						
																									21						
																									22						
																									23						
																									24						
																									25						
																									26						
																									27						
																									28						
																									29						
																									30						
																									31						
																									32						
																									33						
																									34						
																									35						
																									36						

SUBJECT TIME/PERIOD	ASSIGNMENTS	WEEK					WEEK					WEEK					WEEK					WEEK				
	DAY	M	T	W	T	F	M	T	W	T	F	M	T	W	T	F	M	T	W	T	F	M	T	W	T	F
NAME	DATE																									
	1																									
	2																									
	3																									
	4																									
	5																									
	6																									
	7																									
	8																									
	9																									
	10																									
	11																									
	12																									
	13																									
	14																									
	15																									
	16																									
	17																									
	18																									
	19																									
	20																									
	21																									
	22																									
	23																									
	24																									
	25																									
	26																									
	27																									
	28																									
	29																									
	30																									
	31																									
	32																									
	33																									
	34																									
	35																									
	36																									

WEEK					WEEK					WEEK					WEEK					WEEK						DAYS PRESENT	DAYS ABSENT	TARDIES			
M	T	W	T	F	M	T	W	T	F	M	T	W	T	F	M	T	W	T	F	M	T	W	T	F							
																									1						
																									2						
																									3						
																									4						
																									5						
																									6						
																									7						
																									8						
																									9						
																									10						
																									11						
																									12						
																									13						
																									14						
																									15						
																									16						
																									17						
																									18						
																									19						
																									20						
																									21						
																									22						
																									23						
																									24						
																									25						
																									26						
																									27						
																									28						
																									29						
																									30						
																									31						
																									32						
																									33						
																									34						
																									35						
																									36						

SUBJECT

TIME/PERIOD

ASSIGNMENTS

		WEEK					WEEK					WEEK					WEEK					WEEK				
	DAY	M	T	W	T	F	M	T	W	T	F	M	T	W	T	F	M	T	W	T	F	M	T	W	T	F
NAME	DATE																									
	1																									
	2																									
	3																									
	4																									
	5																									
	6																									
	7																									
	8																									
	9																									
	10																									
	11																									
	12																									
	13																									
	14																									
	15																									
	16																									
	17																									
	18																									
	19																									
	20																									
	21																									
	22																									
	23																									
	24																									
	25																									
	26																									
	27																									
	28																									
	29																									
	30																									
	31																									
	32																									
	33																									
	34																									
	35																									
	36																									

WEEK					WEEK					WEEK					WEEK					WEEK						DAYS PRESENT	DAYS ABSENT	TARDIES			
M	T	W	T	F	M	T	W	T	F	M	T	W	T	F	M	T	W	T	F	M	T	W	T	F							
																									1						
																									2						
																									3						
																									4						
																									5						
																									6						
																									7						
																									8						
																									9						
																									10						
																									11						
																									12						
																									13						
																									14						
																									15						
																									16						
																									17						
																									18						
																									19						
																									20						
																									21						
																									22						
																									23						
																									24						
																									25						
																									26						
																									27						
																									28						
																									29						
																									30						
																									31						
																									32						
																									33						
																									34						
																									35						
																									36						

SUBJECT

TIME/PERIOD

NAME	DATE	WEEK					WEEK					WEEK					WEEK					WEEK				
	ASSIGNMENTS																									
	DAY	M	T	W	T	F	M	T	W	T	F	M	T	W	T	F	M	T	W	T	F	M	T	W	T	F
	1																									
	2																									
	3																									
	4																									
	5																									
	6																									
	7																									
	8																									
	9																									
	10																									
	11																									
	12																									
	13																									
	14																									
	15																									
	16																									
	17																									
	18																									
	19																									
	20																									
	21																									
	22																									
	23																									
	24																									
	25																									
	26																									
	27																									
	28																									
	29																									
	30																									
	31																									
	32																									
	33																									
	34																									
	35																									
	36																									

WEEK					WEEK					WEEK					WEEK					WEEK						DAYS PRESENT	DAYS ABSENT	TARDIES			
M	T	W	T	F	M	T	W	T	F	M	T	W	T	F	M	T	W	T	F	M	T	W	T	F							
																									1						
																									2						
																									3						
																									4						
																									5						
																									6						
																									7						
																									8						
																									9						
																									10						
																									11						
																									12						
																									13						
																									14						
																									15						
																									16						
																									17						
																									18						
																									19						
																									20						
																									21						
																									22						
																									23						
																									24						
																									25						
																									26						
																									27						
																									28						
																									29						
																									30						
																									31						
																									32						
																									33						
																									34						
																									35						
																									36						

SUBJECT

TIME/PERIOD

	ASSIGNMENTS	WEEK					WEEK					WEEK					WEEK					WEEK				
	DAY	M	T	W	T	F	M	T	W	T	F	M	T	W	T	F	M	T	W	T	F	M	T	W	T	F
NAME	DATE																									
	1																									
	2																									
	3																									
	4																									
	5																									
	6																									
	7																									
	8																									
	9																									
	10																									
	11																									
	12																									
	13																									
	14																									
	15																									
	16																									
	17																									
	18																									
	19																									
	20																									
	21																									
	22																									
	23																									
	24																									
	25																									
	26																									
	27																									
	28																									
	29																									
	30																									
	31																									
	32																									
	33																									
	34																									
	35																									
	36																									

WEEK					WEEK					WEEK					WEEK					WEEK						DAYS PRESENT	DAYS ABSENT	TARDIES			
M	T	W	T	F	M	T	W	T	F	M	T	W	T	F	M	T	W	T	F	M	T	W	T	F							
																									1						
																									2						
																									3						
																									4						
																									5						
																									6						
																									7						
																									8						
																									9						
																									10						
																									11						
																									12						
																									13						
																									14						
																									15						
																									16						
																									17						
																									18						
																									19						
																									20						
																									21						
																									22						
																									23						
																									24						
																									25						
																									26						
																									27						
																									28						
																									29						
																									30						
																									31						
																									32						
																									33						
																									34						
																									35						
																									36						

SUBJECT

TIME/PERIOD

		WEEK					WEEK					WEEK					WEEK					WEEK				
	ASSIGNMENTS																									
	DAY	M	T	W	T	F	M	T	W	T	F	M	T	W	T	F	M	T	W	T	F	M	T	W	T	F
NAME	DATE																									
	1																									
	2																									
	3																									
	4																									
	5																									
	6																									
	7																									
	8																									
	9																									
	10																									
	11																									
	12																									
	13																									
	14																									
	15																									
	16																									
	17																									
	18																									
	19																									
	20																									
	21																									
	22																									
	23																									
	24																									
	25																									
	26																									
	27																									
	28																									
	29																									
	30																									
	31																									
	32																									
	33																									
	34																									
	35																									
	36																									

WEEK					WEEK					WEEK					WEEK					WEEK						DAYS PRESENT	DAYS ABSENT	TARDIES			
M	T	W	T	F	M	T	W	T	F	M	T	W	T	F	M	T	W	T	F	M	T	W	T	F							
																									1						
																									2						
																									3						
																									4						
																									5						
																									6						
																									7						
																									8						
																									9						
																									10						
																									11						
																									12						
																									13						
																									14						
																									15						
																									16						
																									17						
																									18						
																									19						
																									20						
																									21						
																									22						
																									23						
																									24						
																									25						
																									26						
																									27						
																									28						
																									29						
																									30						
																									31						
																									32						
																									33						
																									34						
																									35						
																									36						

SUBJECT TIME/PERIOD	ASSIGNMENTS	WEEK					WEEK					WEEK					WEEK					WEEK				
	DAY	M	T	W	T	F	M	T	W	T	F	M	T	W	T	F	M	T	W	T	F	M	T	W	T	F
NAME	DATE																									
	1																									
	2																									
	3																									
	4																									
	5																									
	6																									
	7																									
	8																									
	9																									
	10																									
	11																									
	12																									
	13																									
	14																									
	15																									
	16																									
	17																									
	18																									
	19																									
	20																									
	21																									
	22																									
	23																									
	24																									
	25																									
	26																									
	27																									
	28																									
	29																									
	30																									
	31																									
	32																									
	33																									
	34																									
	35																									
	36																									

WEEK					WEEK					WEEK					WEEK					WEEK						DAYS PRESENT	DAYS ABSENT	TARDIES			
M	T	W	T	F	M	T	W	T	F	M	T	W	T	F	M	T	W	T	F	M	T	W	T	F							
																									1						
																									2						
																									3						
																									4						
																									5						
																									6						
																									7						
																									8						
																									9						
																									10						
																									11						
																									12						
																									13						
																									14						
																									15						
																									16						
																									17						
																									18						
																									19						
																									20						
																									21						
																									22						
																									23						
																									24						
																									25						
																									26						
																									27						
																									28						
																									29						
																									30						
																									31						
																									32						
																									33						
																									34						
																									35						
																									36						

SUBJECT TIME/PERIOD	ASSIGNMENTS	WEEK					WEEK					WEEK					WEEK					WEEK				
	DAY	M	T	W	T	F	M	T	W	T	F	M	T	W	T	F	M	T	W	T	F	M	T	W	T	F
NAME	DATE																									
	1																									
	2																									
	3																									
	4																									
	5																									
	6																									
	7																									
	8																									
	9																									
	10																									
	11																									
	12																									
	13																									
	14																									
	15																									
	16																									
	17																									
	18																									
	19																									
	20																									
	21																									
	22																									
	23																									
	24																									
	25																									
	26																									
	27																									
	28																									
	29																									
	30																									
	31																									
	32																									
	33																									
	34																									
	35																									
	36																									

WEEK					WEEK					WEEK					WEEK					WEEK						DAYS PRESENT	DAYS ABSENT	TARDIES				
M	T	W	T	F	M	T	W	T	F	M	T	W	T	F	M	T	W	T	F	M	T	W	T	F								
																									1							
																									2							
																									3							
																									4							
																									5							
																									6							
																									7							
																									8							
																									9							
																									10							
																									11							
																									12							
																									13							
																									14							
																									15							
																									16							
																									17							
																									18							
																									19							
																									20							
																									21							
																									22							
																									23							
																									24							
																									25							
																									26							
																									27							
																									28							
																									29							
																									30							
																									31							
																									32							
																									33							
																									34							
																									35							
																									36							

SUBJECT TIME/PERIOD	ASSIGNMENTS	WEEK					WEEK					WEEK					WEEK					WEEK				
	DAY	M	T	W	T	F	M	T	W	T	F	M	T	W	T	F	M	T	W	T	F	M	T	W	T	F
NAME	DATE																									
	1																									
	2																									
	3																									
	4																									
	5																									
	6																									
	7																									
	8																									
	9																									
	10																									
	11																									
	12																									
	13																									
	14																									
	15																									
	16																									
	17																									
	18																									
	19																									
	20																									
	21																									
	22																									
	23																									
	24																									
	25																									
	26																									
	27																									
	28																									
	29																									
	30																									
	31																									
	32																									
	33																									
	34																									
	35																									
	36																									

WEEK					WEEK					WEEK					WEEK					WEEK						DAYS PRESENT	DAYS ABSENT	TARDIES			
M	T	W	T	F	M	T	W	T	F	M	T	W	T	F	M	T	W	T	F	M	T	W	T	F							
																									1						
																									2						
																									3						
																									4						
																									5						
																									6						
																									7						
																									8						
																									9						
																									10						
																									11						
																									12						
																									13						
																									14						
																									15						
																									16						
																									17						
																									18						
																									19						
																									20						
																									21						
																									22						
																									23						
																									24						
																									25						
																									26						
																									27						
																									28						
																									29						
																									30						
																									31						
																									32						
																									33						
																									34						
																									35						
																									36						

SUBJECT

TIME/PERIOD

ASSIGNMENTS	WEEK					WEEK					WEEK					WEEK					WEEK				
DAY	M	T	W	T	F	M	T	W	T	F	M	T	W	T	F	M	T	W	T	F	M	T	W	T	F
NAME / DATE																									
1																									
2																									
3																									
4																									
5																									
6																									
7																									
8																									
9																									
10																									
11																									
12																									
13																									
14																									
15																									
16																									
17																									
18																									
19																									
20																									
21																									
22																									
23																									
24																									
25																									
26																									
27																									
28																									
29																									
30																									
31																									
32																									
33																									
34																									
35																									
36																									

WEEK					WEEK					WEEK					WEEK					WEEK						DAYS PRESENT	DAYS ABSENT	TARDIES			
M	T	W	T	F	M	T	W	T	F	M	T	W	T	F	M	T	W	T	F	M	T	W	T	F							
																									1						
																									2						
																									3						
																									4						
																									5						
																									6						
																									7						
																									8						
																									9						
																									10						
																									11						
																									12						
																									13						
																									14						
																									15						
																									16						
																									17						
																									18						
																									19						
																									20						
																									21						
																									22						
																									23						
																									24						
																									25						
																									26						
																									27						
																									28						
																									29						
																									30						
																									31						
																									32						
																									33						
																									34						
																									35						
																									36						

SUBJECT TIME/PERIOD	ASSIGNMENTS	WEEK					WEEK					WEEK					WEEK					WEEK				
	DAY	M	T	W	T	F	M	T	W	T	F	M	T	W	T	F	M	T	W	T	F	M	T	W	T	F
NAME	DATE																									
	1																									
	2																									
	3																									
	4																									
	5																									
	6																									
	7																									
	8																									
	9																									
	10																									
	11																									
	12																									
	13																									
	14																									
	15																									
	16																									
	17																									
	18																									
	19																									
	20																									
	21																									
	22																									
	23																									
	24																									
	25																									
	26																									
	27																									
	28																									
	29																									
	30																									
	31																									
	32																									
	33																									
	34																									
	35																									
	36																									

WEEK					WEEK					WEEK					WEEK					WEEK						DAYS PRESENT	DAYS ABSENT	TARDIES			
M	T	W	T	F	M	T	W	T	F	M	T	W	T	F	M	T	W	T	F	M	T	W	T	F							
																									1						
																									2						
																									3						
																									4						
																									5						
																									6						
																									7						
																									8						
																									9						
																									10						
																									11						
																									12						
																									13						
																									14						
																									15						
																									16						
																									17						
																									18						
																									19						
																									20						
																									21						
																									22						
																									23						
																									24						
																									25						
																									26						
																									27						
																									28						
																									29						
																									30						
																									31						
																									32						
																									33						
																									34						
																									35						
																									36						

GRADING CHART

Total Number of Items

	1	2	3	4	5	6	7	8	9	10	11	12	13	14	15	16	17	18	19	20	21	22	23	24	25	26	27	28	29	30
50	98	96	94	92	90	88	86	84	82	80	78	76	74	72	70	68	66	64	62	60	58	56	54	52	50	48	46	44	42	40
49	98	96	94	92	90	88	86	84	82	80	78	76	73	71	69	67	65	63	61	59	57	55	53	51	49	47	45	43	41	39
48	98	96	94	92	90	88	85	83	81	79	77	75	73	71	69	67	65	63	60	58	56	54	52	50	48	46	44	42	40	38
47	98	96	94	91	89	87	85	83	81	79	77	74	72	70	68	66	64	62	60	57	55	53	51	49	47	45	43	40	38	36
46	98	96	93	91	89	87	85	81	80	78	76	74	72	70	67	65	63	61	59	57	54	52	50	48	46	43	41	39	37	35
45	98	95	93	91	89	87	84	82	80	78	76	73	71	69	67	64	62	60	58	56	53	51	49	47	44	42	40	38	36	33
44	98	95	93	91	89	86	84	82	80	77	75	73	70	68	66	64	61	59	57	55	52	50	48	45	43	41	39	36	34	32
43	98	95	93	91	88	86	84	81	79	77	74	72	70	67	65	63	60	58	56	53	51	49	47	44	42	40	37	35	33	30
42	98	95	93	90	88	86	83	81	79	76	74	71	69	67	64	62	60	57	55	52	50	48	45	43	40	38	36	33	31	29
41	98	95	93	90	88	85	83	80	78	75	73	71	68	66	63	61	59	56	54	51	49	46	44	41	39	37	34	32	29	27
40	98	95	93	90	88	85	83	80	78	75	73	70	68	65	63	60	58	55	53	50	48	45	43	40	38	35	33	30	28	25
39	97	95	92	90	87	85	82	79	77	74	72	69	67	64	62	59	56	54	51	49	46	44	41	38	36	33	31	28	26	23
38	97	95	92	89	87	84	82	79	76	74	71	68	66	63	61	58	55	53	50	47	45	42	39	37	34	32	29	26	24	21
37	97	95	92	89	86	84	81	78	76	73	70	68	65	62	59	57	54	51	49	46	43	41	38	35	32	30	27	24	22	19
36	97	94	92	89	86	83	81	78	75	72	69	67	64	61	58	56	53	50	47	44	42	39	36	33	31	28	25	22	19	17
35	97	94	91	89	86	83	80	77	74	71	69	66	63	60	57	54	51	49	46	43	40	37	34	31	29	26	23	20	17	14
34	97	94	91	88	85	82	79	76	74	71	68	65	62	59	56	53	50	47	44	41	38	35	32	39	26	24	21	18	15	12
33	97	94	91	88	85	82	79	76	73	70	67	64	61	58	55	52	48	45	42	39	36	33	30	27	24	21	18	15	12	9
32	97	94	91	88	84	81	78	75	72	69	66	63	59	56	53	50	47	44	41	38	34	31	28	25	22	19	16	13	9	6
31	97	94	90	87	84	81	77	74	71	68	65	61	58	55	52	48	45	42	39	35	32	29	26	23	19	16	13	10	6	3
30	97	93	90	87	83	80	77	73	70	67	63	60	57	53	50	47	43	40	37	33	30	27	23	20	17	13	10	7	3	
29	97	93	90	86	83	79	76	72	69	66	62	59	55	52	48	45	41	38	34	31	28	24	21	17	14	10	7	3		
28	96	93	89	86	82	79	75	71	68	64	61	57	54	50	46	43	39	36	32	29	25	21	18	14	11	7	4			
27	96	93	89	85	81	78	74	70	67	63	59	56	52	48	44	41	37	33	30	26	22	19	15	11	7	4				
26	96	92	88	85	81	77	73	69	65	62	58	54	50	46	42	38	35	31	27	23	19	15	12	8	4					
25	96	92	88	84	80	76	72	68	64	60	56	52	48	44	40	36	32	28	24	20	16	12	8	4						
24	96	92	88	83	79	75	71	67	63	58	54	50	46	42	38	33	29	25	21	17	13	8	4							
23	96	91	87	83	78	74	70	65	61	57	52	48	43	39	35	30	26	22	17	13	9	4								
22	95	91	86	82	77	73	68	64	59	55	50	45	41	36	32	27	23	18	14	9	5									
21	95	90	86	81	76	71	67	62	57	52	48	43	38	33	29	24	19	14	10	5										
20	95	90	85	80	75	70	65	60	55	50	45	40	35	30	25	20	15	10	5											
19	95	89	84	79	74	68	63	58	53	47	42	37	32	26	21	16	11	5												
18	94	89	83	78	72	67	61	56	50	44	39	33	28	22	17	11	6													
17	94	88	82	76	71	65	59	53	47	41	35	29	24	19	12	6														
16	94	88	81	75	69	63	56	50	44	38	31	25	19	13	6															
15	93	87	80	73	67	60	53	47	40	33	27	20	13	7																
14	93	86	79	71	64	57	50	43	36	29	21	14	7																	
13	92	85	77	69	62	54	46	38	31	23	15	8																		
12	92	83	75	67	58	50	42	33	25	17	8																			
11	91	82	73	64	55	45	36	27	18	9																				
10	90	80	70	60	50	40	30	20	10																					
9	89	78	67	56	44	36	22	11																						
8	88	75	63	50	38	25	13																							
7	86	71	57	43	29	14																								
6	83	67	50	33	17																									
5	80	60	40	20																										
4	75	50	25																											
3	67	33																												

Number of Incorrect Items